When Pigs Fly

With love,
Lisa

When Pigs Fly

And Other Insightful Thoughts

Lisa Farrell

Writers Club Press
San Jose New York Lincoln Shanghai

When Pigs Fly
And Other Insightful Thoughts

Writers Club Press
an imprint of iUniverse, Inc.

For information address:
iUniverse, Inc.
5220 S. 16th St., Suite 200
Lincoln, NE 68512
www.iuniverse.com

Any resemblance to actual people and events is purely coincidental.
This is a work of fiction.

ISBN: 0-595-21832-6

Printed in the United States of America

Contents

Stories

Forward

God has blessed me with the ability to help others see His blessings when the blessings are, shall I say, subtle. My humor is at times quirky, but it comes from the true joy that overflows in my soul. It is a childhood dream to have this book in print and I cannot stop praising God for this opportunity.

The book is a combination of poetry and short stories. The stories are true stories from my life. I do not mention very many people by name in my stories. The names are not necessary and this saves embarrassment for many people. If you see yourself in any of these stories, just ask yourself if we have ever crossed paths.

The poetry is a collection of my poems written over many years. There are even a few I wrote in grade school. Some are very expressive and deep. Other poems are, well, they are pretty-darn- simple. There is a message to each and every one. So, sit back and enjoy the experience that awaits you. You may actually need to lie down!

Acknowledgments

I have to start by thanking God for all the superior blessings that He fills my life with everyday. He has given me a family like no other! God definitely had a plan when he joined Bobby and I in marriage. I have never before experienced or seen such a unique and amazing love. My children are next in line on the thank you list. They have brought so many wonderful things into my life. I never imagined that what the world sees as handicapped is actually on open door to heaven. Thank you to my mother, brother and step-dad as well. They had to listen to me ramble about each poem and story for several months. And thank you to anyone brave enough to actually read this book. May God bless you!

A New Life

Your spirit soars as you hear the word baby.
You look the same now, but you know that will soon change.
It's hard to believe that a new life is forming inside your womb.
Each breath supplies more than just support for you now.
You take special care to do all the right things.
Each week gets you closer to meeting the person for whom you already care about so deeply.
The tiny feet press against your stomach for a sensation like no other.
To experience life within your body is a precious gift that only God can give.
As the new life emerges into this world you truly see the smile of heaven.
It's amazing to see a person with your traits and characteristics that is still so completely unique.
What a joy! What a gift to experience!
A new life.

A Tower

I stand alone, rather small, but misperceived
I appear as a tower or at least I must
A stronghold of stability for everyone
Each rope that anchors to me has a weight of its own
Some float with ease and some I must pull
Each pull tears a little more down
The hand that holds me holds me strong
I stand as a tower for it is my job.

Adoption Poem

Not flesh of flesh,
Or bone of my bone,
But still miraculously my own.
Never forget for a single minute,
You didn't grow under my heart,
But in it.

An Ending

Is it a bright light or just stillness?
Do you start in a new beginning or
Do you replay what has already been?
Is glory ever present?
The flying that was impossible, does it become real?
Are you a god or mated with the Almighty forever?
Does it become an instant change or is there quiet in
between?
Is it an ending at all, or just the beginning of what was to be
all along?

Andrew

He does not hear me call his name, but yet
he smiles at me.
He does not know to call me mother, but yet
he knows that's who I am.
His world is silent, but yet he laughs
Can he hear himself laughing?
He cannot speak to express himself, but yet
he makes himself known.
I long to hear him say, "Mommy, I love
you.", but yet he does it everyday.
He tells me by his smile when he sees me.
He tells me by the tears when he wants to be
held.
He tells me by not being satisfied unless
with me.
For you see though he does not speak and
does not hear,
The Lord exchanges our love so that he hears
it and speaks it to me in his own way.

Family

This is an interesting word.
It means mostly people that you cannot choose.
It is a strong word.
It carries weights that normally would be cast down very early.
So much comes from family, and yet we try to leave it behind.
What has been discarded by some, has been the missing piece to others.
It is the foundation for whole empires, and yet crumbles with a few mischosen words.
It should mirror God's love.
Family.

Gardenias

I smelled the gardenias
and missed you so much
I could hardly breathe
I walked into the house
and there you were
standing at the kitchen sink
like a million times before
You were smiling
Knowing the scent of those flowers
would make me want you back
so desperately
You said, "yes I'm here"
and I felt so safe and warm
and comforted
Then I awakened
and the weight was resting
on my heart again
Now I love you and the
Gardenias.

Happy Anniversary

The past two years have held a lot
And that's a fact!
We've gotten married, moved four times,
Had two kids and not looked back.

We've purchased a car
And a house you see.
So it's really no wonder
We've filed for bankruptcy.

We've learned a lot about
How to hope and how to love.
We've even learned
About things like Spina Bifida.

We've had many trials
Some we've failed and some we've passed.
The Lord tries to show us daily
That our love is meant to last.

In this world where
People break up everyday,
The Lord has given us commitment
And His spirit to lead our way.

The past two years
Hasn't even made a dent,
In the life we will share
And in the years we will have spent.

I'm so proud of you
And I love being part of your life.
My joy began two years ago
On the day I became your wife.

He Awakens

He awakens sharply
And he looks around,
He sees no security
Can be found.

He is frightened and scared
As he stares into the dark,
He hears many noises
A distant dog barks.

He longs to express
Just how he feels,
But he knows no words
So he lets out a squeal!

He sees a person
Towering over his head,
He recognizes the man
Standing next to his bed.

He knows this man will keep
Him safe from all harm,
He longs for the touch
Of his father's strong arm.

He cries on dad's shoulder
While dad rocks him to sleep,
His eyes feel heavy
And he lets out a peep.

Safe again at last
And so calm is he,
It's amazing what love can do
When it comes from daddy.

Joshua

As I sit and watch you
still, quiet, peaceful, resting,
but only for a while
By some wonderful miracle
I know you'll awaken
You'll be well
Even more so than before
Healed by one touch
That's greater than any other
Strong by means I cannot see
But that are so evident
As I sit and watch you
I know there will be that moment
when your smile will come
and laughter will follow.

Joy

It is simple and pure
A smile, a glance
It is deep and involved
It requires a choice
It happens without warning
It cannot be measured
It is a window into heaven
To some it seems to always be touchable
To some it seems impossible to reach
It is always present, just sometimes unseen.

Justice

Is it justice when a man of color, who has committed a crime, is captured, yet another man commits the same crime and goes free?
Is it cause for question that the majority of people behind bars are black? Is it just chance or does "justice" have skewed vision?
Will we ever see the scales of justice truly equal?
I pray justice will be colorblind. I pray that the blindness will start now and that it will start with me.

Life

Life is so fragile, we should handle it with care.
We often just rush through with no time to spare.

We see people around us, but don't take the time,
To give them a moment or just a spare dime.

The children watch t.v. to learn the values that they need.
Then we ask why they hate and their hearts are filled with
greed.

We must learn to love our brother no matter what the cost.
We must stop all the violence, just look at all we've lost.

Means of Grace

I take a breath and find all of my strength gone.
For a moment I am tired. I am really tired.
Then I cry out to the Lord, "Fill me Father. Fill me with your strength."
I am silent.
The calm comes. The crying ceases.
I am still.
I feel the arms of grace.
They are strong and enveloping.
I am swallowed for a moment. I am released to breathe.
The renewal is present.
The pain is still here, but it is far less demanding.
It has been stifled by the grace of the one who created the mountains and causes the wind to cease and makes the waves rise and calm.
Praise be to God!
The God of the here and now. God in the highest.

Mom's Advice

Don't talk to strangers.
And be sure to look both ways.
Never run with a sucker in your mouth.
And don't bring home strays.

Don't run up and down bleachers.
And please don't climb that tree.
Never tell anyone your parents aren't home.
And do not argue with me.

Always chew your food good.
And use your manners all the time.
All the advice mom gives is great.
But please, I'm 29!

Music of my Heart

The music of my heart grows with so many things, my kids,
my husband, a soft, gentle rain.
The notes get stronger when a flower blooms
When I see the majesty God has created all around.
Laughter adds a sweet note to the song.
I love for my heart to sing on and on.

My Children

I look at my children with awe.
These tiny people that have been entrusted to me
I am to form their minds and shape their values
Their future partially rests in my hands.
Do they feel loved? Do they feel secure and valued?
This is my responsibility and blessing.
I am supposed to help them grow, but it seems that they are
teaching me.
Thank you Lord for the gift of children.
Thank you for the glimpse of heaven that they bring.

My Haikus

The sky turns dark
Thunder booms
The lightning splits the sky
A harsh summer storm.

The smell so sweet
Colors so brilliant
Wild flowers blooming in the field.

It whispers softly
Through the trees
Cools you off
A soft, warm, summer breeze.

A Limerick

There was an old book in a case.
Who said, "it's those people I face!
They rip up my bind
They hurt my poor spine
Oh why do they do such disgrace?"

Written in 6th grade—Lisa G Cole (Farrell)

My Heart's Pleasure

My heart's pleasure is simple indeed.
He's strong and handsome and in every way does please.

My heart's pleasure can only be one
He loves me and cares for me 'til the day is done.

My heart's pleasure is a desire I must have, I couldn't breathe
without him
He's the one God planned just for me, and I was planned
just for him.

Our Country

I'm proud of the flag that I salute.
My country is strong and unique.
I am a woman and I can do anything that I can dream.
I am not restricted in what I can believe.
I have a voice and I can use it.
I have the freedom to raise my children as I see fit.
I am privileged enough to relax in my living room, to sleep
in a new bed, and to have a refrigerator to store a supply of
food.
Thank you to all the men and women who have fought for
my freedom.
Thank you to those fighting even now.
I pray that I will always recognize the blessing of life in
America.

She Came To Me

A broken spirit she came to me
So lonely, bruised, and battling.

The walls were thick, but with little holes
The light was dim, but came from her soul.

Her smile, at first, was charming and sweet
But it lacked the true joy that a child should feel.

Her years are but six and her mind only three
Yet she knows too well all the worlds misery.

So we start to mend the brokeness and pain
Each day we keep peeling the layers away.

The bright little girl is beginning to shine
The joy is unspeakable, hers and mine.

Suzanne

I spoke to God today
And thanked Him for making you.
He smiled as He told me
That He wasn't quite yet through.

He said everything in life
Has molded us as friends.
He gave us the love,
And the friendship we must tend.

He knew my life would have
Special needs and cares.
So He made you that special person
With whom my heart would share,

All the joys and struggles
For with you, I'm really me.
I praise God that He gave you eyes of love
Out of which to see.

You're someone truly special
God's with you to the end.
I know I've been very blessed by God
To be able to call you friend!

Teri

Today I found an answered prayer
I asked for a blessing
and you were there.
A tower, a beacon, a definite light
Guiding and loving and
persevering and bright.
The strength you display
is amazing, pure, and true
It's as if a window of heaven is
openly shown through you.
The ability to see
through the eyes of love
is a beautiful gift
given only from above.
You are so very special,
giving, and kind
It's an honor and a privilege
to call you my friend!

The Farm

The land is beautiful on the American farm.
The animals wander free.
The cows and goats graze through the grass.
While the barn holds grain and feed.

The pigs roam the pen and wallow in the mud.
While the hens and chickens peck.
The horses gallop around the track.
The farmer fishes off the deck.

The Feet Prayer

Dear Lord, give me compass feet
So that I may always follow your path.

Dear Lord, give me steady feet
So that when the way gets bumpy I will stand strong.

Dear Lord, give me soldier feet
So that I may stand against the enemy with power.

Dear Lord, give me humble feet
So that I will not trip on my own glory.

Dear Lord, give me merciful feet
So that I may forgive others as our paths cross.

Dear Lord, most of all, give me servant feet
That I may show others your love!

The Job

Does it rule your life or just provide for it?
The job.
Does it raise your blood pressure or just give you a raise?
The job.
Does it give you a sense of accomplishment?
The job.
Does it leave you empty and drained or give you joy?
The job.
Does it make you feel proud of what you do?
The job.
Does it contribute to your well being?
The job.
Is it really just work or is it everything in life?
The job.

The Lighthouse

In the darkness a ship roars through the waves.
The water separating at the strength of the vessel.
Nothing stopping the fearless monster.
But darkness hides one thing that can not just damage, but
destroy the glorious ship.
And the one salvation, in the blackest night, is the ray of
light.
It shines a powerful, saving beam that guides the mighty ves-
sel from danger.
One beam. Salvation.

The Soul

Dark and lonely
Full of hope
Shattered, broken, never ending
Dreams begin
Determined, unwavering
Hollow, drained
Overflowing
Life source
Essence of being
Connection to God, brotherhood
Completely unique
The Soul.

To Read

To read is to journey through time or space.
You can travel to places that you will never see.
You have the chance to see life through someone else's eyes.
You can learn foreign languages or cultures not your own.
You can escape to fantasy or help solve a crime.
Time has no boundaries when you read.
A moment in time can be relived for generations if it is written in a book.
A child learns about the world through books.
Regions are explored and planets described in books.
Books change our lives.
Books can make us better people as we expand our minds.

When I Get To Heaven (Josh's Thoughts)

When I get to heaven
I will walk 'round the streets.
I will sit and talk with Jesus
And will dance joyously on my feet.

When I get to heaven
I will bow before God's throne.
I will sing halleluia
Because I will do it on my own.

When I get to heaven
I will run where angels trod.
I will clap my hands together
While I give all the praise to God.

When I get to heaven
I will hold Jesus' hand
I will release the joy my soul has held
And will dance, because I can!

When Pigs Fly

When pigs fly I'll be doing so many things.
I'll write in my journal, keep my house clean, and budget my
money.
When pigs fly I'll write to all my friends to keep them
informed of my daily life.
When pigs fly my laundry will be done on a set schedule.
You will be able to come over anytime and find everything in
order.
When pigs fly I will give my children instructions one time
and the task will be done.
When pigs fly I won't have a headache while I perform the
tasks of everyday living.
When pigs fly I will enjoy cleaning the kitchen and bath-
room and count it a blessing to do so.
When pigs fly I will have my time so organized that I can sit
and relax without feeling guilty because I finished my chores
first.
All of this will happen. Of course it will happen when pigs fly!

Where Is God?

So many people search.
Asking through their circumstance where is God?
Yet God is all around. He's in everything.
They see sickness, not the healing that God provides.
They see heartbreak and ruin instead of strength and stead-
fastness.
If only the eyes of the world would choose to see God.
He is in every breath we take.
He is in the sun and the rain.
He brings the flowers to bloom and gives the birds their
song.
God is all around.
Next time you ask where is God, take a deep breath and feel
Him in your life!

9-11-01

Two towers stood side by side
Hundreds of businesses were within their walls.
Each person walking through the doors with the confidence
that tomorrow will come.
People, worried about being late or the wrinkles in their
shirt, never asking how will I breathe my next breath.
Sitting with a stack of memos and dreading the daily tasks
that lay ahead.
The next moment changes so much about the world.
So many of the unnecessary things of life faded away.
Lives were lost and people were changed forever.
Insecurity, anger, confusion, and resolve emerged.
Two towers stood and now a nation stands tall.

Story #1—A Baby

Bobby and I were very young when we got married (I, of course, was much younger). We had decided to wait 3 or 4 years before we started a family. We were living in a city where we knew no one and to top it off I didn't work outside the home. I actually didn't work inside the home either. This brought about terrible boredom in my life. So I, being the spiritual woman that I am, prayed to God for something to fill my life. As I said before, I was young and hadn't experienced God's sense of humor yet. Several months went by and WOW.... I found out I was pregnant. Being 19 and bored, I thought this would be a great adventure. I would have my very own baby to dress up and play with and cuddle with. How cute! I couldn't wait. I couldn't even hear the first slight chuckle that God breathed because I was caught in my own elation.

The next month, I started to hear a laughter that I wouldn't understand until much later. That God, he's such a kidder! My first doctors appointment went okay, but they couldn't hear the baby's heartbeat. "No big deal," they said, "this happens all the time. We'll just do a sonogram to make sure everything's okay." The doctor said goodbye and told us that the nurse would handle the rest. We went into the sonogram room and waited to see our baby. Wow, our first appointment and we were already going to see our baby. What a blessing! The nurse came in and started the standard sonogram. We saw the heartbeat. The baby looked like a small worm, but I knew that it was already a living human being inside my womb. I was awestruck and excited. Then it happened. The nurse looked a little strange. She just kept moving the wand and staring at the screen. "This is really weird," she said. Her statement made my heart sink. What's wrong with my baby, I thought. The flashing light on the screen looked fine to me. I gathered my strength and asked, "what's wrong?" She just smiled a little and said that the baby seemed to be flipping over as she moved the wand. She then said, "it almost seems like there's two babies in there." We had a good laugh and she went to get the doctor. Bobby and I just looked at each other and we decided that she must be new and not quite used to the equipment yet. The doctor came in and had a look for himself. He turned to us and matter-of-factly said, "yep, it's twins."

That God, he's such a kidder!

Story #2—Me Fisto

When I was a little girl, about eight years old. My family went to church faithfully. We were devoted Southern Baptists. My mother and father both taught Sunday School. They sang in the choir and even tithed. I knew all the "standard" Bible stories. I could sing "Jesus Loves Me" like an angel. I knew that Jesus saved me. I wasn't quite sure what I needed to be saved from, but I knew I should be saved.

I had a friend that lived directly across the street. We loved to play together. She was a few years older than I was, but we were best buds. One Saturday, she asked if I would like to go to mass with her and her family. I couldn't imagine what mass was, but I agreed. My parents said that I could go, so off I went. We sat for several hours listening to her priest. We read our prayers from a book and most of his message was written in a book too. This was quite different from the church service I was used to.

When I returned home I told my parents that my friend was Catholic. I was quite curious as to what my title was. My father proudly told me that we were Baptists and we didn't believe just like the Catholics did.

I had listened to our preacher and I decided that this must mean that she didn't believe in Jesus. I knew that Jesus had instructed us to make disciples of everyone. In my eight-year-old mind, this meant direct confrontation. Since I thought you had to be Baptist to really love Jesus, I asked her to become a Baptist. She refused. I didn't understand. I was offering her this wonderful opportunity, that I had presented so well, and she was refusing. I then turned to the only other persuasive devise that I knew. I told her to become a Baptist or else. She still refused. I then gave her a black eye. Thank goodness God forgives and helps us to realize that when He says that we are His hands and feet, He would prefer if we didn't show people His power through them.

Story #3—Marriage

My husband and I are a true story of love at first sight. He swept me off my feet and I hit him like a Mac truck. One day short of three weeks after our first date he took me out to dinner. It happened to be my birthday so he had flowers waiting at the table. I was beside myself. He was so romantic! We sat through dinner and I talked and ate. He actually looked quite ill through the entire meal. He didn't eat very much and I thought he might get sick at the table. After dinner he finally disclosed the "bug" that was causing his illness. He asked me to marry him. He had just made me the happiest woman in the world. We decided not to wait very long. We planned to be married in just two months. Everything was splendid. God's plan was laid before us and we knew we were listening to His will for our lives. Sometimes, God's will isn't completely free of discomfort.

As the wedding grew closer our excitement grew as well. Everything was falling into place and the road was smooth. It came down to the week before the Big day. I started the week with a sore throat and slight fever, but I just ignored it and prayed that it wouldn't slow me down. The night before the wedding, we had the usual rehearsal with dinner afterwards. We then said goodbye and separated as two separate lives for the last time.

My fever had gone up several degrees and I was now throwing up. I had the full-blown flu. Bummer! I was up all night and I thought I would have to get better to die. However, God provided strength and I made it through the ceremony the next day.

We have always known that our marriage was in God's perfect plan. We do however find humor in the fact that the thought of popping the question made Bobby sick to his stomach and the thought of walking down the aisle made me sick for a week!

Story #4—Backwards

As a small child I always loved to go "antiquing" (that was our term for going to garage sales and junk shops). The one person I could always count on to take me with her was my favorite aunt. (okay, so she's my only aunt, but if I had others, I'm sure she would be my favorite). She loves to browse through shop after shop and barter for the best deal. Saturday morning is her time. She runs errands, goes to libraries and bookstores, and all the "junk" shops. Well, when I was a child I was there with her to do these tasks, but now she does it alone. Don't get me wrong, she's a highly capable, very intelligent woman, but sometimes even she can forget the small stuff. She stopped by our house one afternoon after already having made her Saturday morning stops. She was relaxing when one of us looked down and to our surprise saw that she had been all over town with her pants on backwards.

A few years later, she called me one Saturday to inform me of another blunder. She had gone out that morning to do errands and had made even more stops than usual. She wondered why several people had stared at her strangely as she passed them or talked with them. After getting gas she got back into the car and checked her hair in the mirror. She was shocked to discover her lips lined with a very dark shade of red lip liner and no lipstick. That's right, just the dark red outline of lips had been talking to people all morning.

Story #5—Feelings

My mother is a whole book all by herself, but I'll just tell you a few stories in this book. Let me preface this story by saying that we all have things about us that are odd to someone else; in my mother's case they are just a little more pronounced.

My mother has behaviors that are unique. Her ideas are definitely her own! She came home from the grocery store one evening with a plastic frog that squeaks. It was a toy meant for a small child. This in and of itself was no big deal. She had a dog. Maybe she bought the frog for her dog to play with. Of course my mother has to explain why she bought the frog. It couldn't be something "normal", like a plaything for puppy. No, no, she bought the PLASTIC frog because she felt sorry for it. She had been walking through the freezer section and spotted the frog, "discarded" by someone (probably a child whose mother said no). She bought the frog because she felt it must be cold and lonely in the freezer so far away from the toy aisle. The sad part of this story is that she was really upset about the frog being left cold and alone. So upset that she had to buy it and bring it to her home to take care of it so that it would feel loved.

Story #6—Kindergarten

Even as a young child I shaped the world around me. While my parents worked and my brother went to school, I stayed with my Nanny (my grandmother). I loved staying at Nanny's house. I'm the baby of the entire family and I was spoiled rotten! I was also blessed with an unstoppable will. My father believed in strict discipline, but not a lot stopped me.

Eventually, the day came that I was to start school. Everyone was so excited. Everyone but me, that is. I liked being with my Nanny. I didn't want to work and follow instructions. So I decided I just wouldn't do it. If my mom tried to leave me at school, I wasn't going to stay. She would pull into the parking lot at school and get me out of the car. She would then try to drive away. As I said before, I was very determined, so my five-year-old self would hold onto the car door as she would try to escape. Having no luck on her own after a few days, my mother enlisted the help of the school principal. This worked great, at first. Every morning, at the same time, the principal would meet me and my mother at the doors of the school. He would take my hand and my mother would go to work. He would take me to his office to wait until class would start. It was great! He gave me candy and let me play at his desk. It was almost as much fun as Nanny's house. But then, the bell would ring and my teacher would make me go to class. This is not my idea of fun. So everyday I would play in the principal's office and then I would scream and cry when I had to go to class. Finally, one day, my teacher was fed up with my behavior. She came to me and said, "Lisa, you have thirty minutes to calm down and start working or I'm taking you to the office for swats." I looked her straight in the eye and told her to take me now, because I would not be quiet!

To my credit, that is the only time I ever got in trouble at school. From first through twelfth grade I was a model student.

Story #7—Nanny and The Store

When I was a young adolescent, my mother and my aunt took turns taking my grandmother to the grocery store every Saturday. I would always go with my mom every other Saturday, when it was her turn. My grandmother always went to the same grocery store, no matter what. Most of the people that worked there knew Nanny well. The manager even knew her by name. Everybody loved Nanny, or as they called her, Susie. She shopped the same way every time she entered the store. She always had a list to make her shopping easier. She always started on the right side of the store and worked her way to the left. The idea was to go down every aisle so that nothing was forgotten. Of course, it never turned out that way. We always had to go back across the store several times before we made it to the checkout. One Saturday, we had already been through the store once and we were looking for a particular item she had forgotten. I looked up from my search to ask Nanny a question and made a shocking discovery. I asked Nanny if her neck felt weird. Unsure why I would ask such a strange question, she looked down to see for herself. Her entire bra had somehow fallen "up" and was now above her shirt and around her neck. We both started laughing and couldn't stop. We were laughing so hard we had to sit in the middle of the aisle so that we didn't fall down or wet our pants. My mother moved quickly away from us. She wanted to make sure she was several aisles away so that no one would know that she came with us. We were so loud that the store manager came over and asked us if there was something he could do. We both hurt so bad from laughing that we couldn't answer the question. We just left the store and let my mom stand in the checkout line.

Story #8—Come Again?

My brother has had many adventures in his life. When he was a young teenager, one of his friends moved to a different state. Several months later my brother (J.P.) had the chance to go visit his friend on the farm where he now lived. When J.P. returned from his adventurous weekend he wanted to tell our mom every detail of his trip. He told her about helping with all the daily duties on the farm. He also told her all about the cows his friend owned. He was so excited about helping with the cows. He had even helped Pinkeye Squirtem. My mother had heard some funny nicknames for farm hands, but this one topped them all. Momma asked J.P. to explain whom he was talking about. J.P., confused by the question, said again that he was the one helping. Momma wondered why her son, who is very intelligent, couldn't explain exactly what he was doing or who he was helping. Finally, our dad heard what they were talking about and was able to interpret the story. J.P. had helped his friend squirt eye drops in all the cows' eyes to prevent the condition known as "pink eye". So, in effect, he helped Pink—Eye - Squirt—'Em!

Story #9—Rebellion

I rarely got into trouble growing up. Okay, so that is a stretch, but I was a good kid. My dad was the disciplinarian and my mom definitely wasn't. If my mom said no to something, my brother or myself would just beg until she finally said yes. When my mom and dad divorced I was fifteen years old. My brother and I went wild. No, I didn't go to parties or drink or do drugs. I just decided that I really didn't have to listen to my mother. My big rebellion happened one evening when my mom and her best friend were playing cards at our house. Two of my friends called and wanted me to go with them to see "Good Morning Vietnam". My mother said that it was 9pm and I didn't need to be out that late. Well, I begged and begged thinking she would give in easily. I even told my friends to come over and pick me up because I just knew I could get her to say yes. I was wrong. I begged. I pleaded. Her response was the same. My heart began to pound. I mean, my friends were on their way over. What was I going to do? Well, I continued to try and sway my mom until my friends arrived. When they got there I took the biggest leap against my mother that I had ever taken. I just jumped into the car and told my friend to drive away. After my heart settled down, we had a great time. The movie was funny and we laughed until it hurt. When the movie was over, we went straight home. Luckily, I didn't do anything other than go to the movie. I was nervous about walking through the door at home. I entered slowly and looked around. Everything was quiet. My brother was in the kitchen and my mom's bedroom light was on, but the door was closed. I thought she might be making me sweat it out. About that time, the doorbell rang. I couldn't imagine who in the world would be at our door at midnight. I quickly went to the door to see who was there. As I opened the door I was shocked to see and hear my mom and her friend yelling, "good morning Vietnam". They had followed me to the movie and sat a few rows behind me the whole time. Thank goodness I was where I said I would be, even if I did go completely against what my mom said. The good news is that my mom's ingenuity prevented me from doing that again!

Story #10—The Doodlebug

Yes, even as a young child, I couldn't stand to be outdone. I wanted to be the center of attention, ALWAYS!

One afternoon, while playing at my grandmother's house, my brother, my cousins, and me were collecting doodlebugs. (Some people call these bugs Roly-Polys). We had each found one that we thought was the best of the bunch. We gathered on the front porch to compare our findings. We each held open our hands careful not to loose our precious cargo. Everyone was amazed at my brother's doodlebug. It was the best by far! I couldn't believe it. Mine was supposed to be the best. It had to be the best. So before my three-year-old mind could think, I grabbed my brother's doodlebug and ate it. I felt total satisfaction as my brother ran into the house crying over the loss of his newest prized possession. Victory was mine once again!

The Lord, my God has given me strength. Strength to bear witness to His name. I pray that everything in my life be done with the purpose of directing people to God. May others see Christ in all I do. Let me give, with the purpose of filling the needs around me, not just fulfilling the uneasiness inside myself. I pray, as the days pass, that I will not remain the same and nor should you. The glory of God is spread through each one of us. If you do not give of yourself, the world is missing something vital that God had planned for us. Stay strong in the truth and He will continue to supply your needs. Thank you and may God bless you in amazing ways!

A Child Or A Monster

The smile was so deceiving.

It could mask such darkness.

To see her, one would think of absolute sweetness.

To watch her play, it was hard to think of anything but good.

Then, to hear the laugh, a laugh like no other.

A laugh that hearing it would make you stop and give you chills.

The evil behind that laugh was not describable.

It was the kind of evil you imagine when you think of the most sinister of people.

The violent acts she would take such pleasure in.

It's hard to see her commit such violent acts and think of anything but evil.

How hard is it then to love this child?

Sometimes very hard and sometimes not hard at all. For she is both, child and monster.

L. Farrell

The Wish

I wish love were always enough.

It's not.

I wish I could fix the deep wounds caused by a "mother"

that knew nothing of her role.

I cannot.

I wish the dream of overcoming everything that the

world said we could not overcome would pull us through.

It will not.

I wish my heart would stop breaking at the very thought

of you, alone, surviving.

It will not.

Sometimes no matter how much love is given the wounds

are too deep to heal.

This is a devastating lesson.

L. Farrell

0-595-21832-6